PACKED WITH POISON!

DEADLY ANIMAL DEFENSES

BY **D. M. SOUZA**
ILLUSTRATIONS BY **JACK HARRIS**

On My Own
SCIENCE

M Millbrook Press/Minneapolis

The author is grateful to Laura Burkhart, Reference Librarian at the California Academy of Sciences, for sharing her research expertise on this topic.

The illustrator wishes to thank Lisa Harris for spending so much time helping with the research.

Millbrook Press, Inc.
A division of Lerner Publishing Group
241 First Avenue North
Minneapolis, MN 55401 U.S.A.

Website address: www.lernerbooks.com

Library of Congress Cataloging-in-Publication Data

Souza, D. M. (Dorothy M.)
    Packed with poison! : deadly animal defenses / by D. M. Souza ; illustrations by
Jack Harris.
       p.   cm. — (On my own science)
    Includes bibliographical references.
    ISBN-13: 978–1–57505–877–1 (lib. bdg. : alk. paper)
    ISBN-10: 1–57505–877–4 (lib. bdg. : alk. paper)
    1. Poisonous animals—Juvenile literature. I. Harris, Jack, 1960- ill. II. Title.
III. Series.
QL100.S68 2006
591.6'5—dc22   2005017985

Manufactured in the United States of America
2 3 4 5 6 7 – JR – 11 10 09 08 07 06

*To Trino and Ed and their
unmatched enthusiasm for science*
—D. M. S.

*To Lisa, Jennifer and Jeremy
for extraordinary patience
with the strange life of an illustrator*
—J. H.

A zoo worker is moving a large rattlesnake
out of its cage.
He hears someone call
and turns to see who it is.
Suddenly, the snake's two long fangs
sink into his arm.
The man's arm swells.
Black and purple blood blisters appear.

In another part of the city,

a young girl is chasing a fly ball.

It lands under a row of bushes.

The girl reaches under the plants

for the ball.

She does not see the shiny body

of a black widow spider.

And she does not feel the spider

bite her finger.

But hours later,

sharp pains shoot through her stomach.

Sweat pours from her body.

Both the young girl and the zoo worker

receive medical care and recover.

But they do not forget what has happened.

They learned firsthand just how dangerous

the poison of some animals can be.

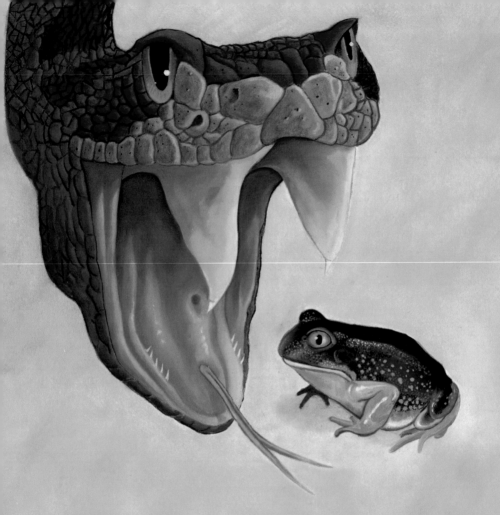

Poison helps many animals
survive in the wild.
They use poison to defend themselves.
Poison also helps them capture prey,
the animals they eat for food.

Rattlesnakes, for example,
have special sacs in their cheeks.
The sacs store a poisonous liquid
called venom.
When a rattlesnake bites an animal,
venom shoots through the snake's fangs.
It goes into the prey.
Soon the prey dies.
The snake swallows the prey whole.

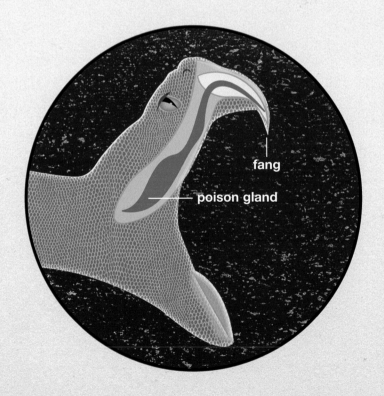

fang

poison gland

duck-billed
platypus

bee

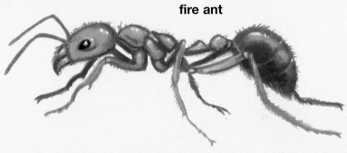

fire ant

Creatures that can inject venom into others
are known as venomous animals.
Not all venomous animals have fangs.
The duck-billed platypus
has a pointed spur on each ankle.
Bees and fire ants have stingers.
These body parts
are just as dangerous as fangs.

Some animals hide poison in their skin
or inside their bodies.
These animals are poisonous.
Eating a poisonous animal
will make a creature sick.
It may even die from the poison.
If the creature lives, it probably won't eat
that kind of animal again.

salamander

Where do some of the most poisonous
and venomous creatures live?
How does their deadly liquid work?
When are humans in danger?
Let's find out.

**Io moth
caterpillar**

Poisonous Animals

In parts of the rain forest
of Central and South America
live brightly colored animals.
They are called poison dart frogs.
Some are tiny enough to sit on a penny.
A few hold poison so deadly that a drop
the size of the period at the end
of this sentence could kill a person.

The frogs' bright colors warn
most hunting animals, called predators,
to stay away.
Some predators that eat the frogs are doomed.
Poison enters their bodies.
Soon they are unable to move.
Their hearts stop beating.
Not even flies or mosquitoes
can safely nibble on these frogs.

Why are these creatures
called poison dart frogs?
People who live in the rain forests
of Colombia used to collect the frogs' poison.
They held the animals over a fire
until a white foam oozed
from the frogs' bodies.
Then hunters rolled
their blowgun darts in the foam.
The hunters used leaves
to protect their hands from the poison.
One frog held enough poison
to coat 50 darts.
The poison remained deadly
for as long as one year.

A puffer fish with poison in many parts of its body is swimming in the ocean. Looking for a meal, a larger fish circles it. The puffer fish takes a big gulp of water and swells like a balloon.

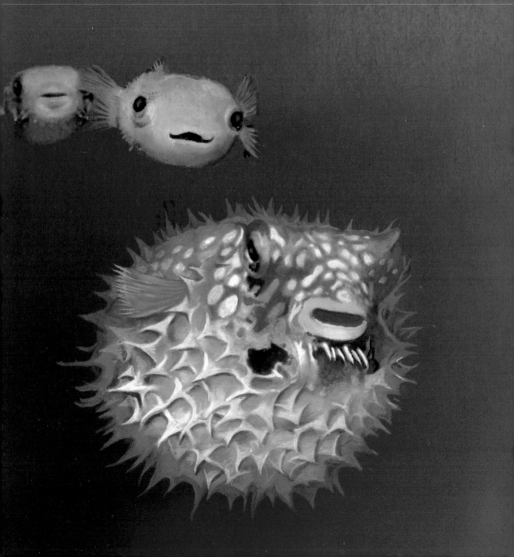

Unable to swallow such a big meal,
the larger fish swims away.
Once danger is gone,
the puffer fish gets rid of the extra water.
It returns to its normal size.

Some people think puffer fish taste delicious.
In Japan, cooked puffer fish is called fugu.
One serving can cost as much as $400.
Cooks are specially trained to remove
every speck of poison from the fish.
If they do not remove it all,
people who eat the fugu
soon have trouble breathing.
Their lips, tongue, and throat may tingle.
Their skin may turn blue,
and their bodies may become stiff.
Their hearts and lungs may stop working.
Each year, 100 to 200 people die
after eating puffer fish that still contain
bits of poison.

Dangerous Fangs

In a garden in India,
a boy discovers a king cobra
sleeping under a shrub.
The snake is as long as a car.
Suddenly, the snake stretches up
until it is almost eye to eye
with the boy.

The snake hisses and spreads its ribs,
making it look as if it is wearing a hood.
The boy backs off slowly
and lets the creature escape under a fence.
The snake does not want to waste its
venom on a creature too large for it to eat.
Instead, the snake saves its venom
to capture other snakes for dinner.

About 500 different kinds of snakes
are venomous.
But most, like the king cobra,
try to avoid humans.
In Australia, a snake called the inland taipan
hides in rat burrows, rock openings,
or cracks in the soil.
It waits for small animals
that move around early in the morning.
The inland taipan's venom
is the deadliest of any land snake on Earth.
This snake's bite has enough venom
to kill 100 people.
But if left alone,
the snake will stay away from people.

Snakes have many ways
to warn other animals to stay away.
Snakes may rise up, hiss, or rattle their tails
to frighten creatures too large to eat.
But most snakes prefer to slither away.

Even if a snake bites,
it may not use its deadly liquid.
Once the venom is used up, it may take
several months to make more.
During that time,
the snake can no longer capture prey.

Venom in the Sea

Along the coast of northern Australia,
a strange, almost invisible creature
floats in the water.
It is a box jellyfish.
The jellyfish's body
is as big as a person's head.
Four bundles of long tentacles
hang below its body.
Each thin tentacle is covered
with millions of venom-filled stingers.
When shrimp or other sea creatures
bump into its tentacles,
the tiny stingers shoot out like spears.
If prey tries to break free,
more stingers jab it.

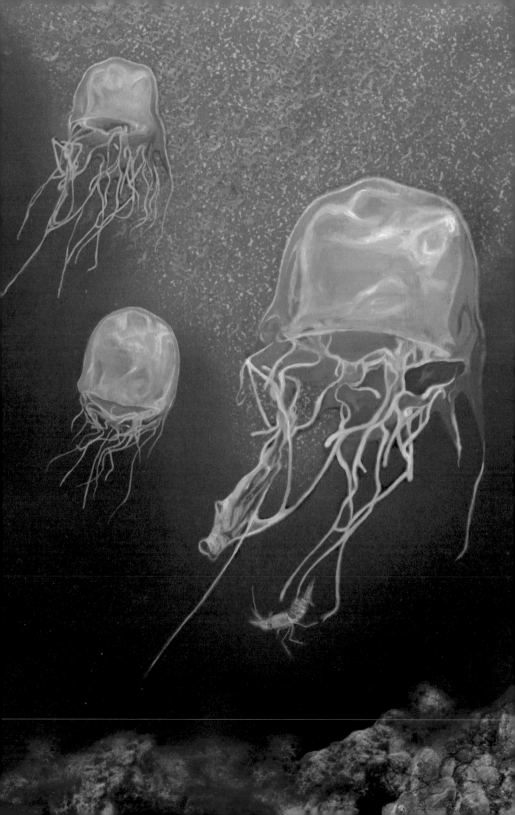

A box jellyfish will also sting
swimmers that brush against it.
More people are killed by box jellyfish
than by sharks and crocodiles combined.
The only animals that can escape
are leatherback turtles and ocean sunfish.
These two sea creatures are much bigger
than a box jellyfish.
They eat the jellyfish
before they can be harmed by its stingers.

Hiding in the sand on the ocean floor
is a stingray.
It is a cousin of sharks.
The stingray has a flat body and one
or more razor-sharp daggers on its tail.
The daggers are for protection.
They cut through flesh and inject venom
into any creature that threatens the stingray.

Stingrays live near coastlines
around the world.
They search the ocean floor for worms,
shellfish, and other small sea life.
When stingrays find a meal,
they cover it with their bodies.
While they eat their treat,
they bury themselves in the sand.
Often only their eyes and tails are showing.

If a swimmer steps on a stingray,
the fish will swing its tail to protect itself.
Its daggers cause a painful wound
that bleeds and swells.
If enough venom enters the wound,
the person's lungs or heart
may stop working.

Tiny Terrors

Spiders live almost everywhere.

Most have venom

that they use to catch prey.

Like snakes, spiders inject venom

through fangs in their mouths.

Their bites are usually harmless to humans.

The spiders either have too little venom

or their fangs are too small.

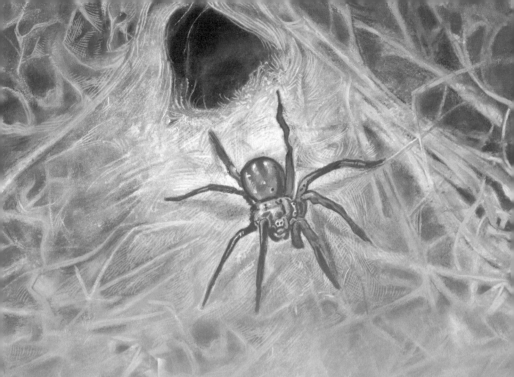

The fangs of the funnel-web spider
of Australia, however, are large and sharp.
They can bite through a fingernail.
Female funnel-webs hide in
cone-shaped globs of silk.
But males wander,
and their bite can be deadly.
These spiders are sometimes called
funnel-web tarantulas.

A black widow spider
may look harmless
as it hangs upside down
on the edge of its web.
But look closely.
A red or orange mark
on its abdomen
tells you that this spider
is dangerous.
Watch an insect land
on its web, and see
how quickly the spider's
venom works.

A black widow
will not usually bite people.
But if it is trapped, it will strike.
The spider's bite is rarely painful.
But a drop of its venom is 10 times
as deadly as a drop of rattlesnake venom.
Someone who has been bitten
should see a doctor as soon as possible.

Scorpions are relatives of spiders.
They live in deserts, forests,
and grasslands around the world.
Some have even been found
under snow-covered rocks
on mountain peaks.
Scorpions hide in dark places
during the day.
They come out at night
to hunt spiders, insects, and other scorpions.
They catch prey in their large pincers.
Then they quickly bend their long tails
over their backs.
Scorpions inject venom
through a stinger on the tip of their tails.

Scorpions often crawl

into houses

and hide in shoes,

clothing, or bedding.

People must be careful

to check places where scorpions

may be hiding.

Scorpions found

in the United States

are usually harmless.

But the death stalker,

which lives in parts of Africa,

can cause serious injury or death.

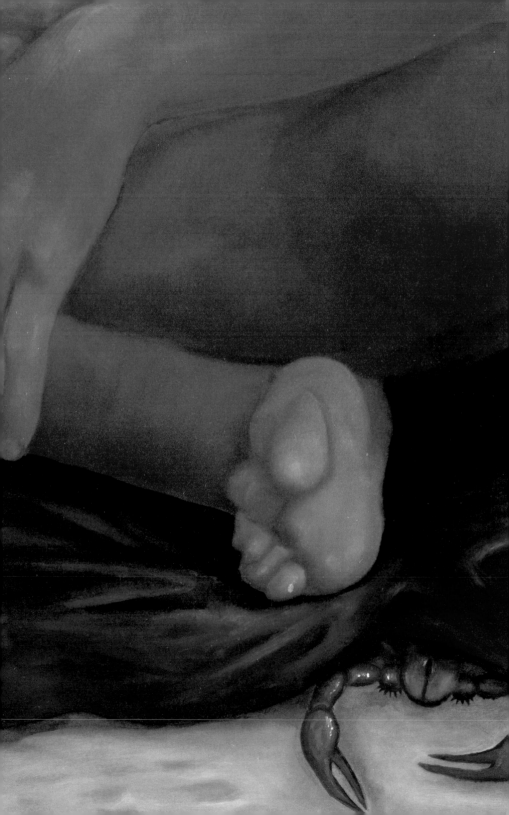

lionfish

Living with Danger

Some of Earth's creatures
can be deadly.
But the venoms and poisons
that make them dangerous
also help them stay alive.

44

These animals do not set out to attack us,
so there is no need to fear them.
Venomous and poisonous animals
simply need space to hunt
and live their lives in the wild.

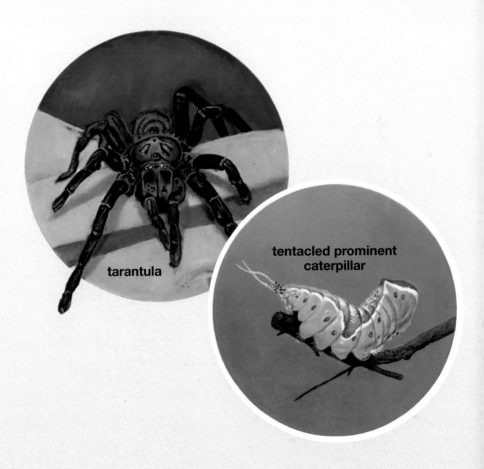

tarantula

tentacled prominent
caterpillar

Lifesaving Venoms and Poisons

A deadly venomous snake has just bitten someone. The person is rushed to the hospital. Doctors begin giving him a lifesaving chemical. It is called antivenin. The word *antivenin* means "against poison." The antivenin slowly stops the snake's venom from attacking different parts of the man's body. In a week, he is well again. Antivenin has saved a life that once would have been lost.

To make antivenin, scientists take venom from some venomous animals one drop at a time. Then the scientists inject a small amount of the venom into another animal, such as a horse or a goat. The blood of these animals produces chemicals that fight the venom. Next, some of the blood is removed from the animal and turned into antivenin. It is stored for emergencies. Sometimes several doses of antivenin must be given to a person.

Scientists have found other ways to put deadly animal venoms to good use. They are learning to use venoms and poisons as painkillers. The venom of scorpions, tarantulas, or other animals may soon help treat illnesses such as cancer and heart disease. In the future, venoms and poisons may do more than help some animals survive in the wild. They may also improve the lives of many people around the world.

Glossary

abdomen (AB-duh-muhn): the back part of an insect's or spider's body

fangs (FANGS): two long, hollow teeth that help animals inject venom. Snakes and spiders have fangs.

pincers (PIHN-churz): claws used for holding prey

predators (PREH-duh-turz): animals that hunt other animals for food

prey (PRAY): animals that are hunted and eaten by other animals

tentacles (TEHN-tih-kulz): long, thin parts of animals that are used for feeling, grasping, or moving. Jellyfish and octopuses have tentacles.

venom (VEH-nuhm): poison made by an animal and injected into its prey

venomous (VEH-nuh-muhs): full of venom, or able to inject venom

Bibliography

Edstrom, Anders. *Venomous and Poisonous Animals*. Malabar, FL: Krieger Publishing, 1992.

Freiberg, Marcos, and Jerry G. Walls. *The World of Venomous Animals*. Neptune, NJ: T. F. H. Publications, 1984.

Hamner, William M. "Australia's Box Jellyfish: A Killer Down Under." *National Geographic* 186 (August 1994): 116–130.

Light, William Haugen. "Eye of Newt, Skin of Toad, Bile of Puffer Fish." *California Wild* 51 (Summer 1998): 8–14.

Slowinski, Joe. "Striking Beauties: Venomous Snakes." *California Wild* 53 (Spring 2000): 30–34.

Sutherland, Struan K. *Venomous Creatures of Australia: A Field Guide with Notes on First Aid*. New York: Oxford University Press, 1994.

Williamson, John A., et al., eds. *Venomous and Poisonous Marine Animals: A Medical and Biological Handbook*. Sydney: University of New South Wales Press, 1996.

Further Reading

Collard III, Sneed B. *Creepy Creatures*. Watertown, MA: Charlesbridge Pub., 1997.

Dewey, Jennifer Owings. *Poison Dart Frogs*. Honesdale, PA: Boyds Mills Press, 1998.

Kite, L. Patricia. *Down in the Sea: The Jellyfish*. Morton Grove, IL: A. Whitman, 1993.

Parsons, Alexandra. *Amazing Poisonous Animals*. New York: Alfred A. Knopf, 1990.

Pascoe, Elaine. *Animals Are Poisonous*. Milwaukee: Gareth Stevens, 2002.

Pope, Joyce. *Deadly Venom*. Austin, TX: Steck-Vaughn Library, 1992.

Storad, Conrad J. *Scorpions*. Minneapolis: Lerner Publications Company, 1995.

Taylor, Barbara. *Poisonous Bugs*. North Mankato, MN: Chrysalis Education, 2003.